DESI MODERN LOVE

An Anthology of
True Stories

Curated by

Ranjani Rao

CONTENTS

FOREWORD

Nandini Patwardhan

The idea of creating an anthology of Indian-themed first-person essays about love came to me over the course of reading the Modern Love column in the New York Times. While I loved the idea of the column, I found that it was somewhat limited in the shades of love that it highlighted.

As a person who has spent well over half my life in the US, I found most of the stories published in the newspaper relatable. Moreover, I found that they exercised my love muscles and increased my capacity to experience love, offer it, and spot it even in mundane everyday interactions.

One example of a compelling story was the decision by the sister of a gay man to carry, through artificial insemination, the baby of his male partner. In this way, the baby would be genetically related to both men. Another example was the story of a long-married woman in Mumbai whose marriage got a lift when she and her husband bonded over nurturing the birds that came to the feeder on their apartment's balcony.

As for "love" in mundane interactions, a highlight of a recent trip to Washington, DC, was the brief conversation I had with the bellhop at the hotel where my friend and I stayed.

"Are you from India?" he asked. "Yes," I said with a smile, "I am from Mumbai."

"It's a big city. Bollywood!" he responded enthusiastically.

Thinking that he might like to share a bit about himself, I asked him where he was from. "Pakistan," he said. He proceeded to tell me of another Indian Punjabi employee of the hotel with whom he had become good friends. "Dono Punjabi Hain. Khoob Baatein Karte Hain." (We are both Punjabis, so we have much to talk about.) By now, the bellhop had resorted to speaking with me in Hindi. He had also resorted to playing the role of a gracious host. It was part of his job to stow my suitcase until I was ready to head to the train station. But, the way he accepted my suitcase spoke volumes.

"I will be here until 3. Come any time!"

And, when I got back, along with my suitcase, he handed me and my friend bottles of water. "Aaj garmi jyada hai, pani rakhiye." (It is hot today, here's some water for your journey.)

The political reality of our two feuding motherlands had been left far behind—as far away as the two countries are from this land that he and I now call home. It was so much easier to be accepting, welcoming, kind, generous, and gracious, than to be defined by acrimony on auto-pilot. It is so much easier to not be indifferent, to engage.

This experience is, to me, a quintessential example of Modern Love—as experienced in the current time and therefore a result of the particular social, cultural, technical, and economic circumstances that exist at this time.

~ ~ ~

The above experience and others like it crystallized for me the limits of the New York Times Modern Love column. Increasingly, the column seems to focus on modern preoccupations such as college dating and hookups, gender identity explorations, and what seem to me shallow explorations of frivolous love.

At the same time, my admittedly nostalgia-fueled memories of my early life in India and present-day interactions with old Indian friends, convince me of the rich trove of love stories that exist in the Indian setting.

While love is an emotion that is universally experienced, it is colored and nuanced by cultural context and setting. At Story Artisan Press, we set out to seek these "desi"-tinted stories, stories shaped as much by the people that give and receive (or not) love as they are by the situations, opportunities, and challenges against which they play out.

We hoped to receive stories about the push-pull of love that exists within and between families, about unexpected friendships on daily commutes, about in-laws, nurturing teachers, dating and arranged marriage in the digital age, and more.

The idea to create an anthology of desi stories was not with the intention to create a walled garden that keeps others out, but from a desire to highlight the stories that take place in a very differently structured culture and society.

This anthology has seven stories. Several relate to love in arranged marriages. The ones that dig deep are about getting married after divorce and feeling love for the mother of one's adopted children. There is a story on in-laws and one about marriage and migration in the modern age.

Publishing this anthology is also an act of "modern love." New technologies have made it possible to reach people in all corners of the world. The contributors to this volume live in India, Singapore, and the US. New technologies have also made it easy to create short books and sell them as e-books. Trees are saved, connections are made, goodwill is extended, opportunities are created, and creativity is expressed.

What could be better?

We are eager to keep this conversation going. Do drop us a note at storyartisanpress@gmail.com. We would appreciate your involvement in our endeavor. Post reviews on book websites, on your blog, and on social media. Send us your own modern love stories. If there is sufficient interest, we would love to publish a second volume.

FACEBOOK FRIENDS

Kalpana Mohan

My husband is a simple, straightforward, and good-natured man. Yet, sometimes, the children and I find it hard to love him in real life. It has become harder still for us to love him unconditionally on Facebook, Gmail, and Google Talk.

Since he built his castle in the virtual world, the eccentricities that once rocked our family—those odd personality quirks of the physical world—are parlaying into seismic faults.

"Hullo parental units, why does Father feel the need to tag his children in every one of their ugly pictures on Facebook?" our daughter pleads on Google Talk. "Why can't Dad let the acne-ravaged, braces-filled past just be?" Meanwhile, our son, a high school senior, has marooned himself on an island on the Internet, far away, where dad cannot find or friend him.

My daily interactions with my husband often revolve around a social networking tool—even when we are at home. Rather than describe something to me, he'll send me a link on Google Talk just so I can read it myself. The precision in our hyperlinked lives is eroding our imaginations, especially when it's amplified by my husband's tendency to over-describe. On Facebook, that character trait can manifest itself as *vishwaroopa*, as when Lord Vishnu aggrandizes into a "super god" of sorts and then proceeds, with one step, to take over the entire universe. The man for whom it's never 245 days, but always 244 days, give or take a few minutes, explains himself too much on Facebook.

His Facebook album of photographs created for a close friend, whom we shall call Shyla, reads as follows:

Shyla-Krish Birthday Party 5-17-2011. The photos in this album, 1 of 2, are from the 50th birthday party thrown by Krish for his wife Shyla at the home of the Kumars in Saratoga on May 17, 2011. For details of the dinner menu go to album ShyJ1.

When he takes photographs of events, for every hour of an event, my husband will shoot about 300 pictures for a minute-by-minute coverage. This endears him to his victims. They feel like celebrities. But what it means for me, the wife, is quite the opposite.

Our domestic life is off-kilter. Friends watch my frustration through the statuses I post on Facebook: "Kalpana Mohan wishes her husband would unload dishes in the dishwasher faster than he uploads photographs onto Facebook." My extreme statuses on the Facebook stage have become a window into our marriage, a marriage that was arranged 27 years ago in Chennai and feels slightly deranged in this age of social networking.

And, oddly enough, through that sheer, droll curtain of my daily pronouncements, some friends have observed what a great couple we make, both on and off Facebook, even though my husband's penchant for transparency has led to civil strife in our home.

Did you know that whenever we go anywhere as a family or as a couple we are checked in, whether we like it or not—at the restaurant, the beauty salon or the coffee shop? I told my husband that some things are best left private: "Kalpana Mohan has told her husband that she does not want to be checked-in while she is in the bathroom."

And so, one day, when I was tired of feeling like a branded iPod at an Apple store sporting a barcode on my derriere, I rebelled. I unfriended my husband. Our Facebook face-off became the subject of conversation among our real and virtual friends; discussion about it spilled into the living rooms of friends.

But it was lonely in my new world. It was inconvenient. I missed talking with my husband about things—a photo, a video or a story—that both of us might have seen. Now, when he was traveling, I couldn't see his updates. As a friend had once quipped, at least I knew what my husband was up to, thanks to Facebook.

I realized, during this time, that Facebook had become another person in our marriage, a warm and fuzzy friend who had become too nosey and intrusive at unwanted times. But the hiatus also made me think about the many ways in which my husband was uniting the community— with his camera and his computer. Thanks to him, we now had a folder of photographs of every friend or relative, alive or dead. Thanks to him, we had memories—of braces, awards, events, and grandparents, warts and all.

While my husband has ticked off some friends and relatives owing to his online mania, our friendships with many others have blossomed because of it. He and his dad have made peace on the social networking platforms. They may be 14,000 kilometers apart but they keep in touch every single day via Gmail, Google Talk, Skype or Facebook.

A few weeks after our Facebook meltdown, I sent my husband a friend request. He ignored it. He snickered to friends. But one morning while he was making himself coffee a few feet away from his laptop, I slunk up. My husband became, once again, my friend.

YOUR MIL IS A MOTHER TOO

Chandrika Krishnan

"Did you order on Amazon?" I ask my husband.

"Yes, 4 pull ups and 4 under-pads," he answers. "Any medicines required?"

Quickly checking, I give a suitable reply.

After thirty-one years of marriage, this is the conversation we have every few days.

Flashback 1988......

My mother was giving the "engaged to be married" me instructions.

"I can never call my mother-in-law, Amma," I said furiously, scowling and muttering angrily at my mother who, like all mothers the world over, bore the brunt of badly behaved children.

"It's only in our Tamil Brahmin community that we call our mother-in-law Amma. She can never be one!"

My long-suffering mother brushed aside my protests with her characteristic "That's the way of life" shrug which rubbed me the wrong way all over again.

Like most others of their generation, my parents were caught in the push-pull of norms dictated by social expectations. They wanted to educate their children to ensure that we were employable and capable of standing on our own if the need arose. At the same time, they wanted to make sure the children were married and "settled" as quickly as possible after they reached marriageable age.

Parents, particularly my own, determined the suitability of a prospective groom based on his finances, family foundation, education, and lineage. But they rarely thought of matters such as compatibility and agreeableness. They expected that, as in most arranged marriages, love and affection would grow naturally thanks to lives lived together.

Educated enough to want the moon—yet not equipped enough to get it—was the youngsters' problem. I was no different.

Closet feminist that I was, the dictates of society failed to persuade me to the virtues of the path my parents wanted for me. I was not brave enough to challenge the norms. Nor was I willing to become the acquiescent young woman that I was expected to be.

~ ~ ~

I was soon married. My after-wedding life followed the most traditional script, in keeping with social and family norms. I became part of a "joint" family. My life became defined by a whole series of subtle and not-so-subtle rules and expectations. I was alternately guided and chastised into falling in line.

Even though I had made peace with my mother's ways, I found that my mother-in-law was much more traditional. She wore a nine-yard sari, which somehow made her seem more authoritarian. She was a formidable cook—her *rasam* was the talk of the town. Intimidated, I was all the more thumbs-and-needles in her presence.

Before long, I realized that my mother-in-law was treating me as her "chief aide." She expected *me to abide by her wishes.* However, she did not think it necessary to pay me even a single compliment. On the contrary, any delay in serving food to the family was attributed to my inability to meet her demands!

All of this was too much for the person that I had been up to this point. Due to my father's poor health, my parents had come to rely on me to handle the many tasks that had to be done in person—bank transactions, train reservations, and mailing letters. *Hence, my culinary skills were limited and just sufficient to feed myself and others who had less exacting expectations.*

Resentment bubbled *within* me

~ ~ ~

That was in 1988. Until 2011, when my mother-in-law breathed her last, she and I had arrived at an uneasy truce. What choice did we have, given that we were both connected to the same man?

I nursed her all through her surgeries. In turn, she turned me into an expert cook.

During those twenty-three years, I had convinced myself that I merely tolerated her. And, I did so out of a sense of duty towards my husband. She was, after all, his mother. However, at the mature age of fifty-three, it has dawned on me that she, too, probably merely tolerated me. I was, after all, her son's life partner. Also, she could hardly forget that she had been instrumental in choosing me as her dear son's wife!

Why then this post?

A popular meme goes like this. "Please don't tell me how to bring up my children, dear mother-in-law. I am living with one of yours and he can sure do with some improvement." But, this meme does not apply in my case.

My mother-in-law's son is a blessing to me, warts and all.

When my father died, it was my husband who performed the last rites and did so with great diligence.

When my mother became very ill, I traveled frequently for an entire year in order to take care of her. My husband did not protest my many absences. Now that she is bed-ridden, she has moved in with us, thanks to his whole-hearted support.

I feel immensely fortunate as well as grateful when I note that my husband is a true family man. He is responsible, loyal, and committed. Over the course of our three-decade long marriage, he has stepped up whenever the situation called for it—financial support, tending to me when I was hospitalized, and helping to take care of our children.

I realize that while I am the beneficiary of my husband's fine qualities, I had absolutely nothing to do with making him the truly wonderful person that he is.

~ ~ ~

It is almost a decade since my mother-in-law passed away. Despite our many differences, I think of her on Mother's Day. I silently thank her for her wonderful son. I wish now that, when I still had the time, I had tried harder to establish better rapport with her. How different might our relationship have been if I had rejected the notion that we would always and only be at cross purposes?

I wish I had been more open-minded and compassionate and not seen all her actions as attempts to thwart me. I wish I had told her what a fine job she did raising her son.

I think back to the young feisty bride that I was and I wish someone had whispered these words of wisdom in my ear.

You and your mother-in-law are more alike than you are different. She too is a woman who left her parents' home and moved in with her in-laws. She, too, put herself second for her family. Be kind and empathetic. Communicate.

There are sure to be disagreements. At such times, extend the olive branch. Never forget that she is the one who is the maker of the greatest gift in your life—the man whom you love and cherish. Don't make your husband choose between yourself and the woman who bore him.

He is your life partner and he is the father of your children. But, he will also always be your mother-in-law's son. Your husband is to your mother-in-law what your son or daughter will be to you.

On Mother's Day, thank that lady who gave you her flesh and blood to call him your own.

A GIANT LEAP FOR WOMANKIND

Surabhi Pandey

When I turned twenty-four, my parents decided that it was time they made "arranging daughter's marriage" as their top goal in life. As with any arranged marriage, entire families were enlisted to convince me that it should be my top priority as well. Although I was young, I knew that marriage would be a giant leap for me. It has always been thus for women—from moving into a new house and adjusting to a different environment, to changing her last name and finding her place in a new family; the institution of marriage was something not be entered into lightly. I was not ready.

I managed to dodge and escape for a year and a half before I caved in. But I made it clear that I would not meet gazillion boys in the dance of acceptance/rejection that plays out in the arranged marriage system. No problem, my parents said, and created a profile for me on a matrimonial portal. I had complete freedom to screen and choose proposals based on my personal preferences. After scrolling through multiple profiles, G was the first boy whose digital proposal I accepted and after two-three months of "courtship" in the virtual world, we decided to tie the knot.

Although still skeptical of marriage, with both of us being based in India at the time of our engagement, we looked forward to the wedding, unaware of the change in dynamics that would occur in a few weeks. G was offered a job in Singapore, an offer that was too good to refuse. This added to my dilemma. I had not considered the possibility of leaving my full and fulfilling life behind to travel abroad to join my husband.

After the wedding, I chose to stay behind in Delhi, ostensibly to take care of pending matters. I had been working as a TV presenter at *Doordarshan* for the past three years and was on the cusp of a promotion. My second book *Saturated Agitation* had recently been launched, and I was busy with book readings across the country. I had just completed my master's degree in journalism, and I was waiting to collect my original mark sheet. I was teaching journalism as a part-time lecturer at a private college and was reluctant to abandon my students in the middle of the semester. One of my dogs had given birth to seven pups. The other one was sick.

Nine months after my wedding, I kept adding more excuses to the already long list of valid reasons for me to linger in Delhi. Despite the distance, G was very considerate in not insisting that I move to Singapore. Was it because he was as tentative as me about our union? Things seemed fine on our occasional short meetings. We connected often over various digital devices and channels. But we did not share a home, we had no history together; whatever we knew of each other was only in bits and pieces, limited by the time we allocated to each other over other priorities. Perhaps we were both too polite and strong-willed to accept that marriage requires physical togetherness to cement our nascent bond.

People often told me how this was a mistake, how I should prioritize my marriage over everything and move to Singapore. Although I did not openly admit to others, I loved the fact that even after marriage, I had this bonus period to live the same old life in my paternal home, surrounded by familiar things, and lead a full life with my television shoots and book readings, journalism classes and press parties. But sometimes in the hours after I completed all the items on my to-do list, on the days when I was truly honest with myself, I acknowledged that this long-distance status of our marriage worried me as well. After all, these were the fleeting, formative years of our marriage and staying apart now could turn out to be too big of a risk.

Plus, I missed my husband. In spite of the obvious limitations, we had grown fond of each other. I learned that he is an amazing man who not only knows how to love and care but also respect me as a partner. I looked forward to our late-night calls and random texts during the day, surprise visits and long-distance gifts but I also worried about getting too comfortable in this situation. And often, my imagination wandered to the unfamiliar country where my husband lived, a place without my family, without pets, without all those things that bound me to Delhi.

~~~

It is the month of August, the month of my husband's birthday. This is his first birthday as my husband, and I do not want us speaking over flat screens looking at each other in buffers and glitches. For some reason, I feel compelled to be with him, I want to make this day special. Is this love?

I make plans, book tickets and buy gifts. I am flying to Singapore tomorrow morning to see him. This is not a surprise visit because I cannot afford the risk of him being elsewhere if I arrive unannounced. I know that G has also made plans—booked a nice suite and reserved fancy dinners. We are both excited to see each other. It has been three months since our last rendezvous.

I weigh my check-in bag, check my cabin luggage and lay out my favorite white cotton *Anarkali* suit for the flight in the morning. I wash my face, kiss my pups and dogs good night, apply night cream and sleep.

I wake up with a mild sense of excitement when my alarm goes off at 4 in the morning. I have to leave home at 5:30 to reach the airport on time. I wear the *anarkali*, straighten my hair and stick on my red *bindi*. I wear the silver bangles that G had bought for me during his last visit and apply kajal.
~~~

I sense a commotion outside our home and the TV news confirms my misgivings.

A sleep deprived, tired and frustrated reporter screams out information about fire, mobs, roadblocks etc. People have turned violent to protest the rape conviction of Baba Ram Rahim who had subsequently been jailed.

Oblivious to the implications of this news, I get ready to leave for the airport only to realize that I cannot step outside. People are walking the streets with swords and fire torches. It is a communal riot–like situation. There are half burnt vehicles on the roads with mobs screaming "*Baba bekasoor hai, Baba ko riha karo*" (Baba is innocent, release him from prison.)

I have a long phone call with G, I don't want to disappoint him. I argue with my father about the unfairness of his demand that I stay home because it is too risky to head out. Before long, I have to accept defeat. There is no way I can safely make it to the airport in time for my flight, thanks to the harsh reality of things beyond my control.

"The important thing is that you are safe at home. It is alright, we can always plan for next month or the month after." G is incredibly sweet and understanding. He is the one consoling me despite the fact that **I** am the one throwing a tantrum for not making it to **his** birthday.

As I sit with my head in my hands, my sick dog walks towards me, lifts his leg and pisses on my bag. And something finally snaps. I have a glimpse of the lesson that I have been trying so hard to not learn. I need to honestly answer the question that has taken root.

"Are the Gods punishing me for not listening to people (and my inner voice) and staying in Delhi? Am I taking advantage of my husband's understanding and supportive nature? Is this a punishment for being a terrible wife? Am I a terrible person?"

The same old answer plays back quickly. *"No No. It is just that I have a lot going on here in Delhi. I have been working as a TV presenter at Doordarshan for the past three years and am at the cusp of a promotion. My second book, "Saturated Agitation", just launched. I am doing readings across the country. I completed my Master's degree in journalism, and I am waiting to collect my original mark sheet. I teach part-time at a private college and my students will feel abandoned if I leave in the middle of the semester. One of my dogs just..."*

But now the words seem shallow and incomplete.

I see my father leaving for his clinic despite the unruly situation outside, knowing that there may be additional patients who need his help. I have grown up seeing him devote his entire life to the welfare of the people. He has been treating patients for free for as long as I can remember. His clinic consultation fees are just Rs. 50 in a city like Delhi. His passion for his work and dedication towards helping others has been an inspiration for me. My father is my hero.

Being the youngest one in the family, I was naturally close to my father. What I hadn't realized was how interdependent we had become in the past few years. I am so much like him. His preoccupation with work had always kept him away from family. Am I doing the same thing? As a married woman, don't I have another life waiting for me once I wake up from this illusion? Am I not supposed to start my new life? To henceforth wear the visage of a married woman?

A woman's life changes entirely after marriage and so does her opinion of it. Before marriage, my focus was more on the "wedding"—clothes, jewelry, make up, events, music and what not. However, the next morning, when the *band baja baraat* was over, I found myself transformed from the kid of my family to the eldest *bahoo* of my husband's family, a promotion of sorts that required major adjustments to my outlook about my life ahead. With the completion of the rituals of marriage, I had wondered what other literal and figurative changes lay in store, but had not ventured to find out.

Today, thanks to Baba Ram Rahim and his crazy followers, I can finally see that it is not my career nor my dogs, not my students nor my mark-sheet holding me here. I got married and was 'given away'. From *kanyadaan* to *bidai*, every ritual confirmed my departure from my maiden home and guided me towards the road to becoming a wife. The only thing that is holding me in my old home, my old set up, my old life, is me. I haven't mustered the strength to leave my father, my home, and my familiar life and begin a life with my husband in my new home in a new country, to become a wife in the true sense. Only I could correct this unfair situation. I had to let my marriage take shape even though I don't know what that shape would be, even though I had no idea how to create it. It was time to fly.

~ ~ ~

In the next ten days, I resigned from work, completed my assignments as best as I could and started looking for work in Singapore. When G came to Delhi to escort me to Singapore, my father waved a tearful goodbye. I knew then that my father was happy for me—he would not have asked me to go away because he wanted me to take that step by myself. He would be fine, and so would I.

As the aircraft gained momentum and trembled with newfound energies to take off, I felt a gush of overwhelming emotions soaring within me that gave me the courage to start my married life.

Sometimes it takes more than mere rituals for a daughter to accept the position of someone's wife, but it is never too late to start and there is nothing wrong in allowing yourself some extra time to graduate to the idea of being a Mrs. After all, marriage is one small step for man, but a giant leap for womankind.

SECOND TIME AROUND

Ranjani Rao

It is still dark when I wake up in the guest room at my brother's home. "*Can't wait to marry you,*" I had sent the SMS to Aditya at midnight. Trying not to wake up my teenage daughter, I adjust the pleats of the magenta silk sari and fasten the heavy fabric on my shoulder with a safety pin. I wear my favorite pair of gold earrings and slip on a pair of bangles on my hands, dark red from the henna. I can't help but smile at the fact that the same henna also hides the grey in my hair.

I have been a bride before. Half a lifetime ago, to be precise.

~ ~ ~

My long black braid was covered in flowers then. The intricate mehndi design had turned from red to maroon to almost black on my warm hands. "It means your husband really loves you," my giggling cousins had chorused. Eager aunts helped drape the silk on my bony shoulders—an unnatural weight, an unfamiliar costume that I had worn only a few times before this momentous day. Numerous relatives watched closely as my mother escorted me to the sacred fire that would be at the center of the wedding rituals.

My groom's and my family environments, food choices, horoscopes, physical characteristics, and other miscellaneous attributes had been matched following a detailed checklist. We were products of marriages that had been arranged in a similar fashion, marriages that had thrived over spans of over a quarter century. We were more than okay with the manner in which we had been brought together.

The religious wedding ceremony was blessed by astrologers, approved by relatives, and witnessed by friends. Soon after, we had left for America, to begin our married life on a continent far away from interfering in-laws and curious onlookers. The odds for a long happy married life were in our favor. The odds had not accounted for the items that were not on the checklist—a few prejudices, big helpings of individual attitudes, more than a pinch of unspoken dreams for the "ever after." There was no checkbox to indicate whether our personal aspirations and expectations would blend well or curdle into a messy muddle.

~ ~ ~

"You are taking a bold step," was my aunt's response when I told her about my decision to remarry, echoing the sentiments of her generation and the skepticism of a culture where divorce and remarriage are rare events.

Thanks to the eighteen-year-long unhappy saga of my first marriage, I knew my mother's opinion on the subject. "Everyone does not get every single wish fulfilled in one lifetime," she had said a few years ago, after yet another discussion about my troubled marriage. While she had come to support my decision to get divorced, she would have tried to dissuade me from marrying again.

My father, although more traditional, had once responded to my rhetorical question of "what would you say if I wanted to remarry" with a simple "You know what marriage entails. If you are ready for it, it's your choice."

Those conversations were purely academic discussions since such an eventuality was a conjecture at best. Perhaps it is as well that both my parents are not alive to witness the second wedding of their only daughter.

I shake off the dreary thoughts and wake up my daughter and help her with her outfit. Two taxis ferry the handful of people who have come to attend the simple Arya Samaj wedding ceremony on my behalf. "Why is she getting married again?" I am sure the guests are asking themselves the same questions.

Hailing from a cultural mindset that put marriage as the centerpiece of a woman's existence, I had taken a long time to get over the fact that mine had crumbled. After the formal divorce, I had alternated between relief and grief, freedom and fear, exhilaration and exhaustion. There had been anger, sadness, rage, self-pity, and remorse. Instead of wallowing in depression, I had chosen to focus on rebuilding: a safe home, a career that would support my single-mom lifestyle and a respectable reputation.

After my mother's death the same year as my divorce, my father had become my anchor. The vacuum created by his demise four years later had led to the realization that I had a long solitary life ahead. Being busy was easy, being alone was not.

On weekends when my daughter visited her father, I binge-watched *Friends*, ate instant noodles and read *Eat Pray Love*. In the still hours of dusk, every tick of the clock was a portent of the years ahead. I couldn't stop my child from growing up or moving away. I could only create my own life, not stifle hers. Would I find someone willing to share my life? If divorce was unusual in India, remarriage was even more unlikely for a woman in her forties with custody of a teenage daughter.

My parents had arranged my first marriage. I had no dating experience. I was not on Facebook. Online matrimony sites and dating apps were not my thing. Finding one suitable man seemed next to impossible.

One afternoon, over lunch with an old friend, I admitted that my life was good.

"I have my own home, work-life balance and most importantly, peace. But sometimes I wish I had someone to spend the rest of my life with..."

"I know just the person you should meet," he said with a twinkle in his eyes.

~ ~ ~

Aditya came into my life first via email, then phone calls. We shared stories, songs, quotations, favorite books, movie dialogues, quiz questions. When we decided to exchange photographs, he sent me a picture of an ageing movie star with the modest disclaimer that he looked better in person! Our first meeting was awkward. We were in our forties, but we found ourselves tongue-tied despite having bared our souls through text messages. A few meetings later we met each other's children. Neither of us was sure of what we wanted from this relationship.

At a restaurant one afternoon, he sat across the table. A comfortable silence hung between us. A random thought, like a spider's web, took root in thin air.

"If he walks away from me now, I won't know how to handle it."

My heart began to thud. In the months since our meeting, I had come to count on him. I loved his French beard and his easy sense of humor. His idea of a good workout was a strenuous game of squash while mine was gentle yoga. He was an unashamed extrovert and I valued my morning hour of solitude. We both loved to read. We respected the different ways in which we had made peace with our lives thus far. With our individual lives chugging along comfortably in different cities, bringing up our kids with our own support systems, we didn't really have a pressing need to be together. And yet, a part of me was tired of being alone.

"I am not tired of being alone," he said. "I don't *want to be* alone anymore. I have been offered a job in Singapore," he declared.

Was this a proposal?

~~~

A year after our first meeting, I am on the way to my second wedding.

Would my parents have supported my decision to jump into matrimony in midlife by marrying a widower with a daughter? This is not the time to speculate.

Any doubts about the wisdom of my decision are dispelled the moment I see the relief on Aditya's face when I reach the venue, a little late.

"I wondered if you had chickened out at the last minute," he jokes, with his dimpled smile.

"Didn't you get my message?" I ask. The question remains unanswered as I am hurried towards relatives for introduction.

This is a wedding with no checklists, no curious onlookers, no astrological consultations. I have invited the few people with whom I have shared my triumphs, people who would give me a shoulder to cry on instead of handing me a gift. I want a ceremony where the marriage endures long after the flowers wither, the music stops and the guests leave.
~~~

An older woman presides over the ceremony with a light-hearted touch. She explains the significance of the rituals. Our girls sit on the stage, a few feet behind us. They are wearing the *ghagras* that we had selected on a joint shopping trip a few weeks earlier, when they had first met.

My older brother and sister-in-law take on the role of the elder family members on my side. As my sari *pallu* is tied to Aditya's outfit, I feel a sense of relief, of belonging, of togetherness. We garland each other and walk around the fire. And finally we are married. There is laughter and blessings, photographs with family and friends.

~~~

I am once again a married woman. On the threshold of a fresh beginning. I have been here before. Everything is different this time. I am twice as old as I was then, my slate is cluttered with history. Major life experiences, not just the heavy silk sari, rest on my no-longer-bony shoulders. My parents are conspicuously absent.

I am reminded of a popular ad for a jewelry brand Tanishq, where a dusky bride walks to her wedding ceremony holding her little girl's hand. As the bride and groom walk around the ceremonial fire, the groom picks up the little girl, thus including the child in the commitment to the new life with her mother. How wonderful for a woman to get a second chance with a man who is willing to accept her child as well, I thought! But I couldn't help wonder what happens once the camera fades away?

I will have to find out for myself.
~~~

The first time around, a twenty-two-year old me had eagerly embraced the novelty of married life in a faraway place. This time, given our ages, Aditya and I, despite having survived our share of shattered dreams and heartbreaks, are trying again. Although we belong to a generation of Indians brought up in stable families, we have witnessed the collapse of this familiar structure within our own lives.

We know what marriage entails, what we expect of each other. We need to be sure what our responsibilities are towards the two daughters we have inherited from our previous marriages. And the families of their parents. There are no guide books or advice for how one must tread on this path. Nor any role models. But we are committed to doing the best we can by each other and our daughters.

As a first, significant step, we have chosen to move to another country to start over. I am aware of the challenges of moving to a new country. Aditya will begin a new job. I will have to find one. The girls, from being the center of the parent's universe, will have to get used to the reality of having a sibling and a step-parent at home and making friends in a foreign country. Add to this mix puberty, teenage angst, midlife crises, personal and professional challenges and I can foresee interesting times ahead.

Maybe fairy tales do come true. In life as in stories, there comes an opportunity to walk into the sunset with the person you love. It doesn't matter if the chance comes the second time around. The difference lies in welcoming that opportunity notwithstanding the doubts and uncertainties.

Two days later I see the email Aditya had sent me the night before the wedding. "*As we are taking a brave step towards a new life, I am sure you have your share of apprehensions and fears. But know this—I will be there every step of the way, even if I am sounding unsure, insecure, joking, or not serious. I am dead serious about making this work— I just know it will.*"

I take a deep breath and surrender to the pure joy of anticipation, the promise of a second chance at marital happiness, with a spouse of my choosing.

Aditya's unambiguous commitment, not to the institution of marriage, but to me is the best gift; words to boost my confidence for the journey that I was about to begin, with a companion who was clear and firm about our goal and what we have chosen—a life of togetherness, with each other and our "plus ones" in a home that we will create in a new country, away from concerned but curious eyes and well-meaning but unasked for advice.

~ ~ ~

Five years later.

You never say you love me, I accuse Aditya almost every night. On a family holiday in a remote village in Iceland, in a tiny hotel bedroom, my pearl earring drops to the wooden floor and disappears. It's not expensive but it was a gift from Dada, who hadn't lived long enough to see my second wedding, so different from the one he had arranged. In these five years, I had often wondered if he would have approved. I frantically search for the lost earring. Aditya joins. Moves furniture. Brings a flashlight. The earring remains hidden. On the drive to the waterfall, he squeezes my hand. I know Dada would have approved.

ACCEPTANCE

Nandini Patwardhan

Prakash and I came to know each other when we were both sixteen. We attended the same coaching class for our high school examination. After that we ended up going to the same college for two years. We parted ways when he chose the biology track, and I chose the mathematics one.

He would often visit me at my house and we would chat for an hour or so. While we chatted, my mother and grandmother would be about. One or the other of them would sometimes join the conversation.

On a couple of occasions Prakash asked me to go out with him. This was the late 1970s in Bombay, a time when social mores were far different than they are today. So, quaint as it may seem now, I asked my mother's permission. She did not exactly say "yes," and she did not say "no" either.

She explained that our society placed a high value on a girl's "good name"—purity and virtue. If people in the community saw me with a male friend, they might draw incorrect conclusions about my character. It would be worse if I later became friends with other boys from college and was seen going about with one or other of them. The compromise that my mother suggested was that I invite Prakash to come to our home as often as he felt like (or I wanted).

Being a creature of that time and place, my mother's suggestion made sense to me. I was neither resentful nor disappointed. If anything, I was glad that she explained her reasoning instead of bluntly censuring me.

One of the last times that Prakash and I met was when he asked me to marry him. I said "No" on the spot. At the tender age of eighteen, I had unarticulated ideas about what kind of life I hoped to live. I had already learnt that the society did not generally offer second chances. So, it was better to be patient, to keep one's heart and options open, and continue to dream in the tiny space available after complying with family and social expectations.

I see now that I was holding out for a more worldly and dynamic man. In contrast, Prakash was a peer, a mere boy.

Having been weaned on the Hindi movie version of romantic relationships, I doubt either Prakash or I had an understanding of romantic love and about the stages of courtship. We probably expected three discrete and uncomplicated stages unfolding in quick succession—profess love, get engaged, get married. So, even when he said "marriage," he was probably not thinking much beyond "go out with me." Maybe, he thought that suggesting marriage would make it easier to overcome my mother's objections. Little did he know that my mother would have also disapproved of pairing up at such a young age.

~~~

Prakash and I soon lost touch. I went away for graduate studies, then worked abroad and got married. These types of casual relationships were the first casualty of the move to the United States. I was too busy making my way in the new world to think of those left behind. Plus the means of communication that we take for granted today, such as email and Whatsapp, were simply not an option.

On the first couple of visits back, I thought I might like to look up Prakash as well as other school and college friends. But, those visits were overwhelming with jet lag, illness, and taking care of the little ones. All plans made during the run-up to the visits mostly remained just plans, and I never got around to looking up any of my friends.

~~~

Fast forward twenty-five years. The internet had opened a dizzying array of possibilities. I received an email message from Prakash, as he had found me through one of my web sites. How did you know it was me? I asked him, for I use my married last name. When you got married, I had seen the notice in the Times, he wrote back.

That was my mother's doing.

I think it is pretty ironic that she, who put a gentle brake on my friendship with Prakash, ended up being the enabler of his finding me again.

~ ~ ~

After we reconnected, he emailed me almost every day. His messages were forwards of photographs, slideshows, or short movies. They ranged from the comic to the spectacular. Since I am not a forwarder, I could not return the favor. I responded to just the messages that I found particularly striking.

Over time I became accustomed to receiving email messages from Prakash. I came to see them not as impersonal thoughtless forwards but as little pings that said, "I thought of you today" or "I think you will like this one."

The mostly one-way and unbalanced nature of our communication did not seem to bother Prakash. But, the unfairness of the lopsided communication bothered me. On several occasions I gently told him that I may no longer be the person he thinks I am. We were just eighteen when we last knew each other. And, over the course of the decades spent in a foreign land, I know that in many respects I have become a foreigner, a stranger to the old ways.

But his faith in me was unshaken. He continued to send messages with little expected in return. And so, I came to have faith not in myself, but in his faith in me. The messages let me feel less alone when loneliness engulfed.

It was nice to know that there was this one person who was able to see me as the original, essential, and organic me. It was nice that unlike many other old relationships, this one was not filtered through the America prism, or refracted by the distance or the two-decade long gap.

We were not competitive as eighteen-year-olds, even though it was a time when most of our peers were. We weren't competitive even after we reconnected. So, rather than inflating our situations, we were honest and we applauded as well as commiserated.

Despite all this (or maybe because of all this), a part of me worried about appearances and propriety. I was studiously careful, making sure my emails neither suggested nor promised specialness.

But, knowing that I would have been far more responsive upon reconnecting with a long-ago girlfriend, I allow myself to be a tad more responsive than my own standards of propriety dictate. And, allowing that this may be the universe's way of deploying an angel my way, I stopped resisting the angel.

~ ~ ~

When I was in college, I was certain that I would not do well in biology because I was not good at drawing illustrations. On the other hand, mathematics concepts seemed to reveal themselves to me with very little effort. So, I chose mathematics as my major.

When I told Prakash my choice of major, he said it was a choice with no future.

"Why?" I asked.

"Because there is no Nobel prize in Mathematics."

"It's not like I am going to be capable of winning the Nobel even if there was one for mathematics," I replied.

Another time, returning from college on the bus, he told me about the big computer company in America. IBM. "I could never get to America," I told him. "A person has to be really smart to get there." It seemed too far-fetched on many levels.

Although I was a diligent student and earned top grades, my humble nature did not allow me to imagine that I had what it took to reach the top and to have spectacular success.

Neither could I imagine that I would defy my parents and go abroad for higher studies. I knew they would worry about the chances of finding a "suitable boy" who would be willing to marry a young woman who had lived by herself in a foreign country. Of course, this reasoning was never articulated. It just hung in the air, like particles of polluting dust. And because it was unexpressed, it also could not be discussed or refuted.

And so I brushed aside IBM and America as so much bravado. As it turned out, the next few years made the idea of America seem within reach, then plausible, then within reach and, finally, real.

Now, decades later I wonder. In those pre-internet days, how did Prakash come to know of IBM and the Nobel prize?

~~~
~~~

I feel amazed that we were both unaffected by cultural norms that would have limited my options. He did not hesitate to suggest spectacular achievements to his female classmate; he did not see me as less deserving or less capable because I was a girl. My expectation of modest achievement was based on an incorrect understanding of what it took to make those giant leaps; but, I too did not see my gender as the limiting factor.

We were both high-achieving students. So, why did he wish these things for me, and not for himself?

~ ~ ~

We went out for coffee on my next visit back. I asked him what he remembers of the type of youngsters we were. What were our hopes and dreams? Did we discuss politics? Were we idealistic? Did we talk about books and movies? I imagined that having lived his entire life where we grew up, he would remember better than I do.

I was trying to understand my emergent self, figure out the influences that subtly shaped me. Who was I and who were we as a people that led to me becoming the person I am today? Maybe the urge to dwell on the past, and try to make sense of it, is a peculiarly American obsession. As far back as 1758—decades before there was a United States of America—Benjamin Franklin (the American Founding Father) made a pilgrimage to England to uncover his ancestors and understand the society in which they lived.

Unfortunately Prakash was unable to engage in this conversation. He could not offer a cookie trail back to where I began. Even so, the fact that we were able to communicate as easily as when we were teenagers was a kind of cookie trail in its own right.

I asked him why he feels such a connection to me. "I don't know... even when we were in college, when I was with you, I felt happy, and my depression lifted," he said. I didn't even know he felt any stress or depression, or even that there was such a thing.

And yet, now, this undemanding, non-judgmental, and enduring childhood friendship is the one that lifts *my* spirits.

MOTHERHOOD CLEAVED

Lakshmi Iyer

cleave: split or sever (something), especially along a natural line or grain. "the large ax his father used to cleave wood for the fire"

cleave: stick fast to. "Rose's mouth was dry, her tongue cleaving to the roof of her mouth." adhere strongly to (a particular pursuit or belief). "part of why we cleave to sports is that excellence is so measurable"

Mother's Day dawned with an excited giggle near my ears.

"Mommy! Mommy!"

I opened my eyes to the sight of two nearly identical faces peering over mine. My eyes crusty from too little sleep and sticky from burrowing under the comforter battling an unusually cold stretch for May, I stretched my arms out for a hug. Instead, I found two handmade cards thrust into my face.

I lingered over them, the stick figures mimicking our family. Two heads with blonde hair, three with black. One plump and the rest emaciated. The lettering alternating between block and cursive, the misspellings achingly adorable. Happy Mother's Day both proclaimed with hearts strewn around the border.

We hugged for a long time before my youngest, the one born to me, toddled in. All through the morning, my timeline on social media was flooded with Mother's Day wishes. "Be sensitive to those without mothers, those longing to be mothers and those who lost children" exhorted one friend. I debated between a like and a cry reaction on Facebook and settled for a simple like.

In years past, I have dutifully forwarded, shared, and written treatises on why it is important for us to be cognizant of and sensitive to the pain of others. I should know, having trodden that painful path myself.

This year I feel insulated. I watch, hear, agree and move on. My mind harks back to the days when family tiptoed around me. Dinner with friends would start with a toast to moms and I would withdraw into a shell. In my thirties and desperate to be a mother, I was thick in the middle of infertility treatments, each menstrual cycle a roller coaster ending with a thud that left me bruised and battered. I soldiered on, battle-weary but adamant that I would be a mother.

Pulling on a blouse one day, my eyes fell on the purple and blue streaks on my abdomen from the hormone shots and it hit me that I could do it no longer. I gave up on medicine and focused my research on adoption instead. Domestic? International? Foster? The questions were many and my husband and I were limited by our status as permanent residents. Neither wholly accepted nor rejected, we settled on domestic private adoption with an attorney facilitating the process.

When motherhood finally found me at the age of 35, when I went from being childless to the mom of twin toddlers in a week, I embraced all of it. My shiny new iPhone captured my children's first few days in all glory. I clicked as they napped, ate, drooled and crawled. I shot videos of them babbling and sent it to everyone on my contact list.

I mastered the art of the selfie so I would be in those pictures with my children. "My children!" I captioned lingering long enough on the exclamation as if it would convey the miracle that Motherhood was for me. I soaked it all in, the trappings, the joy, the social sanction and most of all the sorority of mothers worldwide.

~~~

I was perplexed when the first Mother's Day a few months into legally being anointed Mother, I felt like a fraud. I grieved on what should have been a day of celebration. I felt walled in, able to see, unable to
~~~

participate. I remembered my twins' first mother—their other mother—and ached for her.

The last image I had of her in my head was of the night we had dinner as a family, a day after we officially became parents of her children. Us, and she with her father and brothers. The conversation was slow, stilted. We centered the conversation on our children hoping that would keep the deep sorrow that permeated the air from swallowing us whole.

I agonized over sending a wish her way. She was a mother and would be one all her life. My children were living proof of that. Was it a day of celebration or mourning? I hesitated as I typed a wish out to her that Mother's Day. Was I being insensitive? If I did not mark the occasion, would that mean I was depriving her of the title of Mom? I dithered and sent out the email. I heard from her days later, simply thanking me and hoping my day was good. I strained to read the scant text, parsing word usage for hidden meanings.

I learned to fake it until one day I made it. I remember the cards, the flowers, the chocolate and, most of all, chubby hands and arms entangled with mine one Mother's Day morning. And, I finally felt like I belonged. I had left my infertile world behind. I claimed my seat at the table even as I acknowledged what was a day of joy for me was a day that the other mother of my children mourned.

Our relationship warmed but I did not dare to ask her, really ask her how she was doing. Did the pictures I send reassure her? Did they remind her of all that she was missing? Was I sharing or was I gloating? There was no rule book, no cues to be had from cold clinical words on my screen.

~ ~ ~

Motherhood for me has been fraught with questions. Each day I mother my children, I compartmentalize, I strive to be the mother I should be to my children. I smother them with physical love, I oil their bodies, the sesame scent pungent, reminiscent of my childhood. I feel my mother as I mother my children, my fingers massaging the skin, yearning for my touch to tell them when words seem insufficient.

I feed them by hand, the texture of food just right, the temperature warm enough. I feed them *pongal* as I was once fed. I am generous with the ghee as my mother instructs me over the phone. I pause as they swallow, adding enough love to the food to heal the fissures that came from being separated from their mother. I worry I am not doing enough to tell them, show them that this life I lead is one I craved for. They were without agency in this decision that changed their lives but what agency I have, I am dedicating it to making sure they remain whole.

Late in the night, I message their mother to check in on her. I read her blog searching for signs she is happy, she is at peace with her decision. Her happiness is central to mine. I realize happiness may be too much to ask, so I settle for peace. The kind of peace that comes from knowing that despite her decision to place her children, they are not lost to her. They belong to her as much as they belong to me.

"Aren't you afraid your children will leave you when they are old enough? What will you do if they move back to their birth family?" These questions eventually come when I speak about our adoption to people we meet socially.

I fall silent trying to understand what the word *leave* means in this context. Can I make them understand that there is no real leaving, that she is family as much as my children are? I usually deflect, changing topics or answering in monosyllables. To very few friends, I explain that I am not insecure, that I view my children (all of my children) as being fellow travelers on my journey in this life. They will all leave eventually I tell them.

~~~

Sometimes, I wonder if I'm really so secure in my capacity to love them or am I guarding my heart, steeling for the eventual separation? I turn to my youngest, a child born from me for answers. My love for her takes a different timbre, it is subdued, it is mind speak, it is soul binding. I quit work after she was born spending an enormous number of hours just physically cuddling her. I know her smell, I know her the way I know myself. The chocolate brown of her skin, the thick, frizzy strands of her hair, the liquid brown pools of her irises, all the little things you know without having to look when you belong.

Often in the adoptive community, there is discussion surrounding positive adoption language. Some claim
~~~

qualifying a child with *adopted* is unnecessary. I find myself nodding as I think all three children are mine in a way they will never be another person's. The adult adoptees claim that the word *adopted* defines their experience and therefore removing it erases their history. I find myself nodding and relating to my cleaved motherhood.

To talk about the dichotomy in the adoption world is like offering yourself up as a target. The law deems the adopted child "as if" born to you and erases all of their birth histories. In the days following the adoption, I struggled with the fact that to receive their amended birth certificates, I would have to send in their original birth certificates. The ones with the name of their mother as their mother. I made copies for my records before mailing them in and getting spanking new ones with my husband and I in them as parents as if they were born to us. Birth parents relinquish their rights in perpetuity, therefore, ensuring that the child is a blank slate upon which a new life is written.

On the other hand, adoptees grow up with a burning need to figure out their identity, all parts of their heritage. They are torn between owing allegiance to the people who raise them and to the people who brought them into the world, never really being told that it is okay to embrace both families.

As a mother who has trouble subscribing to any particular view, I am torn. I want my older children to know the uncomplicated love that my youngest knows and understands but I also feel that it is impossible when you are pulled in many ways.

In my conversation with other adoptive parents, the idea that parents can love many children, therefore, children can love two sets of parents is brought up. In principle, I agree but it is not the same my heart says. There is something inimitable about being cocooned inside another person's body that marks you and them for life. That bond between a baby and the mother cannot be supplanted. It can be supplemented, supported and approximated even but never replaced.

~~~

They are young, still in the process of growing their vocabulary when it comes to expressing adoption grief. I see it in the way the air stills when we talk about their birth family. I see it in the way they claim cards and gifts from their great-grandparents. I see it in the wistfulness when they send messages to their mom. I see it in the way they eye me with my youngest.

"You don't know me from your heart" my oldest child hurled at me one day as we argued about chores. I stopped, struck by her choice of words. I went mute because it hit too close to home. I turned and left and took the time to figure out how to answer. Later that night, I sat on her bed, my ears on her chest, listening to her heart. I promised to listen to her heart and invited her to listen to mine. We finally talked about what was frustrating her and annoying me. The issue was resolved but I walked away with something greater, an understanding that sometimes, it
~~~

takes a little more listening and hearing to understand what my twins say.

The twins and I recently had DNA tests done. We sat in the study, the children flanking me as I described how they were part German, part Native American and, part English. I showed them a map that showed which parts of the world their ancestors came from. They oohed and aahed at the pretty colors on the map. When it came to mine, it was one solid yellow block. "South Asian 99.9%," it read.

Long after that night, we touch upon the concept of race at odd times. They ask. "Where did our German ancestors come from?" "Your mother's father's side," I say. We go back and forth, tracing genealogy and talking about immigration. They take pride in having Native American ancestry. They reach for the picture of their mother and uncles from our last trip to their birthplace from their shelf and notice the similarities.

As much as it is inviting to redefine family as one based on love, to focus on our shared history and experiences, the loss of children to adoption impacts generations. I mourn the loss of parts of their birth family who are unaware of their existence. My heart aches for the missed connections, the lost ties.

~~~

It brings me back to Mother's Day and all of its associated connotations. It makes me wonder about what makes a mother. It makes me focus inward and accept the dichotomy so I can then move forward. By accepting there
~~~

is a difference in the way I connect with my child by birth and my children by adoption, I can attempt to understand how their mother feels. I can try to understand how my children view adoption and the pull they have toward their birth families. It helps me understand why the example of a parent loving many children is not the same as an adopted child loving two sets of parents.

From understanding comes acceptance and progress. It helps me celebrate mothering as an ongoing action as against a one-time incidence of giving birth. It helps me accept that my motherhood is cleaved and that it is okay.

This essay first appeared as part of the anthology titled "I Am Strength" and published by Blind Faith Books.

WHAT'S LOVE GOT TO DO WITH IT?

Sathya Ramaganapathy

Fifteen years. That is how long I have been searching. But I still haven't found what I'm looking for. Ok, I have not climbed the highest mountains or scaled the city walls. But I have run and I have crawled. Well, almost. And I still haven't found what I'm looking for.

Love. Ishq. Pyaar. Kaadal.
I could throw in a few other languages there as well, but that would be showing off. And my mother did not raise me to be like that. But I digress. Love, true love. I know I would recognize it, if I saw it. After all, I'm an expert on love. I've devoured every historical, contemporary and anything-in-between romance I could lay my hands on. I've watched

countless classic, sappy rom com movies of the Hollywood, Bollywood, and Kollywood variety. I know what it would feel like to fall in love, be in love, true love. Your heart in your mouth, your stomach twisted in knots, violins in the background, that strange giddy feeling...

That kind of love. That is what I yearn for.

~ ~ ~

Love at first sight. Eyes meet across a crowded room, and for a moment, a brief moment, time comes to a standstill. Or, that's what they say.

Did I catch my first sight of him across a crowded room? Yes, I did. Only, it is arranged. The parents broached the matter and with no real reason to resist, I have given in to the inevitable. I have given them a checklist to work through. I hope the list will buy me some time. But it doesn't quite work out the way I imagine. In no time at all, they have lined up a "boy" who meets all the conditions on my list.

"He is so tall," I complain.

"That was not on the checklist," they reply.

I insist on meeting him alone. He has agreed to pick me up at my office, just across the road from the Victoria Terminus railway station, VT as it was called then. I walk in to the reception area. All I have is a photo to identify him by, the one the parents have dutifully couriered across. My eyes dart across faces, as I urgently look for a tall guy with a mustache.

Is he the ONE? Yes, he definitely is. No one north of Chennai would sport that big brush of a mustache. Back then all I knew was the toothbrush mustache, made famous by Charlie Chaplin and Hitler. One, a comedian, and another, a tyrant. Not a good omen. I edge closer. I am sure now that it is not a toothbrush. It is thick and wide and has a downward slope that outlines a mouth that stretches into a friendly smile in greeting. It's called a Chevron, I learn later.

Did my heart skip a beat, did time stand still, even for a moment? Nah, at least not then. Yeh hai Mumbai meri jaan, the city that never sleeps. You can forget about time standing still.

I'm sure it was not love.

~ ~ ~

A sultry June morning in Chennai. I've been up since the early hours of dawn, with nothing to sustain me except milk and bananas. What's it with all the milk and bananas they keep force-feeding you in these Tamil weddings? The unfamiliar weight of the heavy Kanjeevaram sari, that a couple of aunts hurriedly help me drape, makes me uncomfortable. I look at the horizontal stripes and fret. What on earth possessed me to pick stripes? They will do nothing for my 5 feet 1 inch tall frame. I think lovingly of my 4 inch heels, bought after a day spent traipsing through every single shoe shop on Linking Road, Bandra. How could I have forgotten that I will not be allowed to wear footwear on the *mandapam*?

The sound of the *Getti Melam* snaps me out of my dazed state. Does he gaze into my eyes lovingly as he ties the *thaali* around my neck? It's hard to say, since I am looking down. Not because I am overcome with shyness. No, I have to bend my head so the others can lift my long braid, heavily laden with flowers, while he ties the thaali. All I think of at that moment is "Dear God, don't let the false braid come off now."

The deed is well and truly done. We are man and wife. The priest asks my husband (how strange that word sounds) to lead me around the fire holding my little finger in his.

"That first touch... your hands must be tingling," cackles an elderly aunt.

"Look at you blush. Don't faint on us now." I hear a distant cousin call out. I remember then why I prefer to keep her at a distance.

Over five hundred guests in the hall, at least a quarter of them crowding around the *mandapam*, is it any wonder that I feel faint. Luckily the moment passes.

I guess it was not love.

~~~

I'm ready to burst. With my news and my bladder. I can't wait for him to come home. He is ecstatic. Even more so than me, if that's possible. He surprises me with a gift. A stuffed doll, a girl in a red polka dot dress, with shaggy hair and cute button eyes. I adore her already.
~~~

He calls every afternoon to ask me how I am doing, a moment carved out of a busy day. He holds my hair back from my face, rubs my back as I throw up, again and again and again. He comes with me to the doctor for every appointment, watches patiently as I devour books and articles that tell me what to expect when I am expecting. He waits for me to demand pickle and ice cream in the middle of the night. Ah, but we live in sleepy Bengaluru and it does not occur to me to put him to test. Missed opportunities.

"He indulges you so much," my friends tell me.

"I'm doing all the hard work here, so he better!" I say, only half-jokingly.

We bring her home, my little poppet. He rushes home eagerly every evening to be with us. With her. I watch him, as he watches her. As he rocks her on his knees, cradling her little frame tenderly in his big palms, all the while talking to her, asking her about her day. Her fingers curl around his thumb trustingly and he gazes at her in wonder. There's a strange heavy feeling in my chest.

"Give her to me" I say abruptly.

He looks up surprised. I almost snatch her from him. I hold her close to me and she latches on happily as the milk gushes out. I feel my chest relax.

Three years later, we do it all over again. From three, we have become four.

Is it love?

Who has time to think of love, when there's a toddler demanding attention and a baby bawling? Waiting to be fed? Burped? Changed? All of the above?

~ ~ ~

"Why are you so angry amma," she asks. She is always so tuned in to my every nuance, this little one of mine.

He looks up from the newspaper, from the crossword puzzle he has been solving with her this Sunday morning. She comes to me and tries to smooth my forehead.

Where did I spring from, this snappy woman with a permanently furrowed brow and a sharp tongue?

"Why do I have to do everything around this house?" I demand, not for the first time. I look around at the mess that is our home. Newspapers strewn all over, books and toys everywhere, clothes lying unfolded, unopened bills and mail, a fine layer of dust on the few surfaces that are not already covered with books and newspapers. Did I already mention the books and newspapers? There is lunch still to be made. I move furiously from room to room, picking things up, putting them away, even as my mind works in a parallel plane, preparing, planning for the week ahead at work.

"Tell me what you want my help with and I'll do it," he says calmly.

"Why do I have to tell you everything? Why can't you see what needs to be done?"

I'm livid. I imagine I look like a bull in a bullfight arena, fire in my eyes, snorting and frothing at the mouth, pounding the ground with my paws. Not a pleasant image, I admit, especially the frothing at the mouth.

I take a deep breath, trying to calm my stressed out nerves.

"There's so much to do. Sometimes I feel like a headless chicken, madly rushing from one thing to the other. This house, the chores, the kids. With all this cluttering my mind, how can I focus on work?"

"But we discussed this when the kids came along. You wanted to take a break from work and get on the slow track. You wanted to take care of them while I focused on work and money," he argues reasonably.

"Yes, it was my choice to take a step back from my career. But I've given ten years of my life for this family and I have nothing left for myself. I hardly have any friends, no achievements to speak of, and my career is a mess. What's gone is gone. I can never get it back," I wail.

"Tell me what YOU want to do and we'll make it work," he says. How can he be so calm when I'm having the mother of all meltdowns?

Love? Bah! Don't even bring up that four letter word.

~ ~ ~

"Why don't you join my running group?" he asks one day.

I look at him incredulously. Long distance running? Me?

"Ha ha, good one. Go pull someone else's leg," I say dismissively.

But he is serious. "You'll like it. I bet you'll make friends there," he says earnestly.

I stonewall him. He keeps at it. Until I give in one day.

"Oh, it's so romantic," gush our friends. "The couple that runs together stays together." Talk about pressure.

I gradually build up the miles. The smiles follow slowly. My first race, my first finish. Who would've thought it? He gifts me a mug with my picture on it—me, with my beaming face and my flying feet. I can't stop smiling. Neither can the kids. Or maybe they are just relieved to see their smiling mother instead of a raging bull.

"Let's do the Mumbai half marathon," he says next.

"Twenty one kilometers? Are you crazy?" I splutter.

"Twenty one point one kilometers," he says helpfully.

"But I can barely run ten kilometers," I say.

"Just turn up for the training and you'll see. You can do it," he says, with more confidence in me than I have in myself.

~~~

Race day. I'm in my sartorial best. Neon orange t-shirt paired with bright pink socks and purple shoes. After all, there's John Abraham to impress right at the start line. Damn, is that his wife next to him? Oh, never mind. Remember, focus. Besides I'm married, and what would the kids say. Tsk, tsk.

I have never undertaken anything this ambitious before. I am almost overwhelmed by the rush of emotions. Who in their right minds would travel eight hundred and forty two kilometers from Bengaluru to Mumbai by air, only to cover twenty one point one kilometers by foot. The early morning breeze cools my strung out nerves. Ganapati
~~~

bappa moriya, they chant, summoning the elephant God to give them the energy for what lies ahead. I hear the steady drum beats of the street performers' dholak, dhamara daka, dhamara daka, dhamara daka dum. My heart picks up the beat and a chill runs down my spine. I'm all warmed up. How can I be warmed up and chilled at the same time?

I run. One foot ahead of the other. One step at a time. I count my steps. One, two, three, four, five, six, seven, eight, nine, ten. And repeat. I want to stop. But giving up is not an option. I must keep going. I must quell the voice that tells me to stop. I will crawl, if need be. But finish I must.

Then I see it. The one iconic image that defines Mumbai. The VT railway station with its towering arches and spires, and the colossal dome with the lady and the torch. Only, it's now called Chhatrapati Shivaji Terminus. But more importantly, it means the end is in sight. I pick up the speed and begin to sprint. My feet fly over the finish line. I am exhilarated.

I walk over to collect my finisher medal. The cold heavy metal feels solid and reassuring in my hand. I have achieved what so many don't even attempt.

I look across the crowd. I feel a strange sense of déjà vu. I'm back to where it all began, fifteen years ago. And then I see him standing there. This tall guy with a big Chevron mustache that no one north of Chennai would sport. He catches my eye and he beams. My legs turn to jelly. My heart pounds furiously. I'm breathless. All normal reactions after finishing a half marathon, I tell myself. I look at him.

At this man whom I've been married to for fifteen years, my life inextricably linked with his. Life.

What's love got to do with it? It's just the endorphins.

This essay was first published in The Madras Mag Anthology of Contemporary Writing.

AUTHOR BIOS

Kalpana Mohan (USA)

Kalpana Mohan's stories, commentaries and humor columns have appeared in NPR, San Francisco Chronicle, San Jose Mercury News, *The Hindu*, Better Homes and Gardens, and other print and online publications. A columnist for India Currents Magazine, Kalpana received fan mail and hate mail for her columns, "On Inglish" and "Desi Lens". The columns also won her a New America Media prize and several San Francisco Peninsula Press Club prizes. Kalpana won a first prize in 2011—and the attention of an agent—at a competition at Kepler's Books in Menlo Park for the best one-minute book pitch; it catalyzed some of her book-length writing projects based on India. Her first book, *DADDYKINS*, a memoir about the last two years with her ailing father, was published in September 2018 by Bloomsbury India. Kalpana's second book, *AN ENGLISH MADE IN INDIA: How a foreign language became local*, will be published by Aleph Book Company in September 2019. Read more about her at http://www.kalpanamohan.com

Chandrika Radhakrishnan (India)

Chandrika R Krishnan has written about one hundred and sixty works of fiction, articles and poems, which have been published in Huffington Post, Good Housekeeping India, The Hindu, The News Minute, Live Mint, India Currents and Quint, among others. Read more about her at https://chandrikarkrishnan.wordpress.com/author/chandrika1306/

Surabhi Pandey (Singapore)

A former TV Presenter at Doordarshan Delhi, Surabhi is the author of "Nascent Wings" and "Saturated Agitation." She is a freelance journalist who focuses on the genres of Tech, Lifestyle, and Social Commentaries. Her work has appeared in numerous media outlets in India and Singapore, including the Times of India, YP SG, Lifestyle Collective, Youth Ki Awaaz, Tech Collective and Re:ad Poetry, among others. She is the founder of The Vent Machine—a digital magazine based in Singapore. Write to her at surabhi2301@gmail.com.

Ranjani Rao (Singapore)

Ranjani Rao is a scientist by training, and a writer by avocation. Originally from India, and a former resident of USA, she currently lives in Singapore. Her essays have appeared in print and digital publications like San Jose Mercury News, Mutha Magazine (USA), The Hindu (India), The Straits Times and Singapore Unbound (Singapore). Her e-books include a collection of essays titled "No longer NRI: How I left America for my homeland; essays on the adventures of resettlement" and "Negative Space and other stories", are available on multiple digital platforms. Ranjani is a co-founder of Story Artisan Press. https://storyartisan.com/ranjani-rao/.

Nandini Patwardhan (USA)

Nandini Patwardhan is a retired software developer. Her writing has been published in the New York Times, and on Slate.com, Alternet.org, Khabar.com, TheHindu.com, and IndiaCurrents.com. Her biography of Dr. Anandi-bai Joshee, India's first woman doctor, will be published in Q4 2019 in English and in Marathi. Nandini is a co-founder of Story Artisan Press. https://storyartisan.com/nandini-patwardhan and https://tobeuseful.wordpress/com.

Lakshmi Iyer (USA)

Lakshmi Iyer is an alumnus of the Yale Writers' Workshop. She has a certificate in creative writing from Simon Fraser University. Her work has appeared in *The Huffington Post, Chicago Now, Mutha Magazine, The Verve, Adoptive Families* and *Women's Web*. Her family is the subject of a documentary on transracial adoption currently in production (@ourdaughtersdoc). She blogs at www.lgiyer.com and is active on Twitter @lakshgiri.

Sathya Ramaganapathy (India)

Sathya Ramaganapathy is a humour writer, blogger, business professional, and a mom. She is the author of the recently published humour book "It's a Mom Thing:

Kickass Parenting" (Rupa Publications), which takes a lighthearted look at navigating the minefield called parenting. Sathya has written three children's books and has been published in Voices from the Attic, The Madras Mag Anthology of Contemporary Writing, literary magazines including Papercuts, Antiserious and The Criterion, and in The Hindustan Times, Deccan Herald and Bangalore Mirror. She blogs at www.thingsmykidssay.in.

REQUEST

If you liked this book, please support us by posting a review on sites such as Amazon and Goodreads.

We love to hear from our readers. So, please drop us a note at storyartisanpress@gmail.com.

With your support, Story Artisan Press will continue to develop and publish thoughtful and thought-provoking books. Please check https://storyartisan.com/books/ for our full listing.

Thank you for your contribution towards building a culture of reading, writing and reflection.

Made in the USA
Monee, IL
07 July 2026

56553674R00042